Presented To:

Laura Mae

Presented By:

Mom

Date:

August 24, 2000

POCKET BIBLE

Honor Books
Tulsa, Oklahoma

WWJD Pocket Bible
ISBN 1-56292-461-3
Copyright © 1998 by Honor Books
P.O. Box 55388
Tulsa, Oklahoma 74155

Been there, done that!

The Bible tells us that Jesus understands our weaknesses, because He was tempted in all the same ways we are tempted. He was and is a man, so He has felt the same emotions, experienced the same fears, and faced the same temptations that we do. He's been there, done that.

Jesus is our example of how to live a good life — a satisfying life. When we keep our eyes on Him, He will show us where to go and what to do. One way we can keep our eyes on Him is to read the Bible. So when you ask yourself, "What Would Jesus Do?" you can always find an answer in the Bible.

The *What Would Jesus Do Pocket Bible* gives you easy-to-find answers from the Bible for the things you face every day. So keep it handy — in your pocket, your locker, or your desk — and you'll have a ready answer for whatever you may face today!

Table of Contents

when I feel:

afraid

Be strong and brave. Don't be afraid of them. Don't be frightened. The Lord your God will go with you. He will not leave you or forget you.

DEUTERONOMY 31:6

wwjd?

I trust you to save me, Lord God, and I won't be afraid. My power and my strength come from you, and you have saved me.

ISAIAH 12:2 CEV

Don't be afraid. I am with you. Don't tremble with fear. I am your God. I will make you strong, as I protect you with my arm and give you victories.

ISAIAH 41:10 CEV

The Spirit that we received is not a spirit that makes us slaves again to fear. The Spirit that we have makes us children of God. And with that Spirit we say, "Father, dear Father."

ROMANS 8:15

afraid

when I'm tempted with:

anger

It's smart to be patient, but it's
stupid to lose your temper.
PROVERBS 14:29 CEV

My dear brothers, always be willing to listen and slow to speak. Do not become angry easily. Anger will not help you live a good life as God wants.

JAMES 1:19-20

The hotheaded do things they'll later regret; the coldhearted get the cold shoulder.

PROVERBS 14:17 THE MESSAGE

Losing your temper causes a lot of trouble, but staying calm settles arguments.

PROVERBS 15:18 CEV

Don't be angry or furious. Anger can lead to sin.

PSALM 37:8 CEV

anger

when it comes to:

attitude

Let the Spirit change your way
of thinking and make you into a
new person. You were created to
be like God, and so you must
please him and be truly holy.

EPHESIANS 4:23-24 CEV

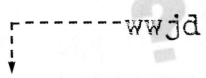

Teach me, and I will be quiet. Show me where I have been wrong.

JOB 6:24

You are God's children whom he loves. So try to be like God. Live a life of love. Love other people just as Christ loved us.

EPHESIANS 5:1-2

Don't be like the people of this world, but let God change the way you think. Then you will know how to do everything that is good and pleasing to him.

ROMANS 12:2 CEV

attitude

when it comes to:

church

You should not stay away from the church meetings, as some are doing. But you should meet together and encourage each other.

HEBREWS 10:25

They followed a daily discipline
of worship in the Temple
followed by meals at home, every
meal a celebration, exuberant and
joyful, as they praised God.

ACTS 2:46 THE MESSAGE

If two or three people come
together in my name, I am there
with them.

MATTHEW 18:20

When they said, "Let's go to the
house of God," my heart leaped for
joy."

PSALM 122:1 THE MESSAGE

church

if I need:

comfort

He is the God of all comfort. He comforts us every time we have trouble, so that we can comfort others when they have trouble. We can comfort them with the same comfort that God gives us.

2 CORINTHIANS 1:3-4

wwjd

But the Holy Spirit will come and help you, because the Father will send the Spirit to take my place. The Spirit will teach you everything and will remind you of what I said while I was with you.

JOHN 14:26 CEV

God is a safe place to hide, ready to help when we need him.

PSALM 46:1 THE MESSAGE

Lord, even when I have trouble all around me, you will keep me alive. When my enemies are angry, you will reach down and save me by your power.

PSALM 138:7

comfort

if I'm feeling:

confused

Trust God from the bottom of
your heart; don't try to figure out
everything on your own. Listen
for God's voice in everything you
do, everywhere you go; he's the
one who will keep you on track.

PROVERBS 3:5-6 THE MESSAGE

r - - - - - - - - -wwjd

God is not a God of confusion but a God of peace.

1 CORINTHIANS 14:33

Where there is jealousy and selfishness, there will be confusion and every kind of evil. But the wisdom that comes from God is like this: First, it is pure. Then it is also peaceful, gentle, and easy to please. This wisdom is always ready to help those who are troubled and to do good for others. This wisdom is always fair and honest.

JAMES 3:16-17

But the Lord God keeps me from being disgraced. So I refuse to give up, because I know God will never let me down.

ISAIAH 50:7 CEV

confused

if I need:

courage

Wait for the Lord's help. Be strong and brave and wait for the Lord's help.

PSALM 27:14

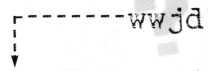

Be brave. Be strong. Don't give up.
Expect God to get here soon.
PSALM 3 1:2 4 THE MESSAGE

Be strong and brave. Don't be
afraid or worried. There is a
greater power with us than with
him. He only has men, but we
have the Lord our God. He will
help us. He will fight our battles.
2 CHRONICLES 3 2:7-8

I've commanded you to be strong
and brave. Don't ever be afraid or
discouraged! I am the Lord your
God, and I will be there to help
you wherever you go.
JOSHUA 1:9 CEV

courage

when it comes to:

dating

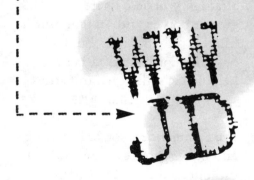

Listen for God's voice in everything you do, everywhere you go; he's the one who will keep you on track.

PROVERBS 3:6 THE MESSAGE

You should know that your body is a temple for the Holy Spirit. The Holy Spirit is in you. You have received the Holy Spirit from God. You do not own yourselves. You were bought by God for a price. So honor God with your bodies.

1 CORINTHIANS 6:19-20

Don't become partners with those who reject God. How can you make a partnership out of right and wrong? That's not partnership; that's war. Is light best friends with dark?

2 CORINTHIANS 6:14 THE MESSAGE

Find a good spouse, you find a good life — and even more: the favor of God!

PROVERBS 18:22 THE MESSAGE

dating

if I'm faced with:

death or loss

But God will destroy death forever. The Lord God will wipe away every tear from every face.

ISAIAH 25:8

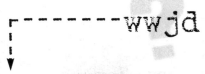

If you practice what I'm telling you, you'll never have to look death in the face.

JOHN 8:5 1 THE MESSAGE

Our dead and decaying bodies will be changed into bodies that won't die or decay. The bodies we now have are weak and can die. But they will be changed into bodies that are eternal. Then the Scriptures will come true, "Death has lost the battle! Where is its victory? Where is its sting?"

1 CORINTHIANS 1 5:5 3 - 5 5 CEV

In times of trouble the wicked are destroyed, but even at death the innocent have faith.

PROVERBS 1 4:3 2 CEV

death or loss

if I'm feeling:

depressed

Is anyone crying for help? God is listening, ready to rescue you. If your heart is broken, you'll find God right there; if you're kicked in the gut, he'll help you catch your breath.

PSALM 34:17-18 THE MESSAGE

Friends, when life gets really difficult, don't jump to the conclusion that God isn't on the job. Instead, be glad that you are in the very thick of what Christ experienced. This is a spiritual refining process, with glory just around the corner.

1 PETER 4:12-13 THE MESSAGE

When you cross deep rivers, I will be with you, and you won't drown. When you walk through fire, you won't be burned or scorched by the flames.

ISAIAH 43:2 CEV

His anger lasts only a moment. But his kindness lasts for a lifetime. Crying may last for a night. But joy comes in the morning.

PSALM 30:5

depressed

when I'm feeling:

discouraged

In everything we have won
more than a victory because of
Christ who loves us.

ROMANS 8:37 CEV

Why are you down in the dumps,
dear soul? Why are you crying the
blues? Fix my eyes on God—soon
I'll be praising again. He puts a
smile of my face. He's my God.

PSALM 4 2:5 THE MESSAGE

If you obey the laws and
teachings that the Lord gave
Moses, you will be successful. Be
strong and brave and don't get
discouraged or be afraid of
anything.

1 CHRONICLES 2 2:1 3 CEV

But you should be strong. Don't
give up, because you will get a
reward for your good work.

2 CHRONICLES 1 5:7

discouraged

if I'm tempted to:

doubt God

The One who called you is
completely dependable. If he said
it, he'll do it!

1 THESSALONIANS 5:24

THE MESSAGE

Surely the Lord's power is enough to save you. He can hear you when you ask him for help.

ISAIAH 59:1

He never doubted that God would keep his promise. Abraham never stopped believing. He grew stronger in his faith and gave praise to God. Abraham felt sure that God was able to do the thing that God promised.

ROMANS 4:20-21

The Lord is not slow in doing what he promised—the way some people understand slowness. But God is being patient with you. He does not want anyone to be lost. He wants everyone to change his heart and life.

2 PETER 3:9

doubt God

if I'm tempted with:

drugs or alcohol

My counsel is this: Live freely,
animated and motivated by God's
Spirit. Then you won't feed the
compulsions of selfishness.

GALATIANS 5:1 6 THE MESSAGE

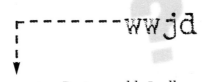

Every time I'm in trouble I call on you, confident that you'll answer.

PSALM 86:7 THE MESSAGE

Stay away from the evil things young people love to do. Try hard to live right and to have faith, love, and peace. Work for these things together with those who have pure hearts and who trust in the Lord.

2 TIMOTHY 2:22

Don't destroy yourself by getting drunk, but let the Spirit fill your life.

EPHESIANS 5:18 CEV

drugs or alcohol

if I face:

failure

When a man's steps follow the Lord, God is pleased with his ways. If he stumbles, he will not fall, because the Lord holds his hand.

PSALM 37:23-24

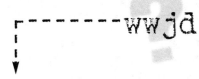

Refuse good advice and watch your plans fail; take good counsel and watch them succeed.

PROVERBS 15:22 THE MESSAGE

Don't be afraid or give up.

JOSHUA 8:1

So, what do you think? With God on our side like this, how can we lose? If God didn't hesitate to put everything on the line for us, embracing our condition and exposing himself to the worst by sending his own Son, is there anything else he wouldn't gladly and freely do for us?

ROMANS 8:31-32 THE MESSAGE

failure

if I need:

faith

Faith makes us sure of what we hope for and gives us proof of what we cannot see.

HEBREWS 11:1 CEV

36

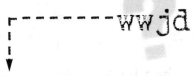

So faith comes from hearing the Good News. And people hear the Good News when someone tells them about Christ.

ROMANS 10:17

It's impossible to please God apart from faith. And why? Because anyone who wants to approach God must believe both that he exists and that he cares enough to respond to those who seek him.

HEBREWS 11:6 THE MESSAGE

You were all baptized into Christ, and so you were all clothed with Christ. This shows that you are all children of God through faith in Christ Jesus.

GALATIANS 3:26-27

faith

when it comes to:

family

The first commandment with a
promise says, "Obey your father
and your mother, and you will
have a long and happy life."
EPHESIANS 6:1-3 CEV

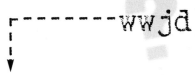

If someone says, "I love God," but hates his brother, he is a liar. He can see his brother, but he hates him. So he cannot love God, whom he has never seen. And God gave us this command: Whoever loves God must also love his brother.

1 JOHN 4:20-21

Don't bad-mouth each other, friends. It's God's Word, his Message, his Royal Rule, that takes a beating in that kind of talk. You're supposed to be honoring the Message, not writing graffiti all over it.

JAMES 4:11 THE MESSAGE

How wonderful, how beautiful, when brothers and sisters get along!

PSALM 133:1 THE MESSAGE

family

if I need to:

forgive

Whenever you stand up to pray, you must forgive what others have done to you. Then your Father in heaven will forgive your sins.

MARK 11:25-26 CEV

In prayer there is a connection between what God does and what you do. You can't get forgiveness from God, for instance, without also forgiving others. If you refuse to do your part, you cut yourself off from God's part.

MATTHEW 6:14-15 THE MESSAGE

But I tell you, love your enemies. Pray for those who hurt you.

MATTHEW 5:44

I tell you, love your enemies. Help and give without expecting a return. You'll never — I promise — regret it. Live out this God-created identity the way our Father lives toward us, generously and graciously, even when we're at our worst. Our Father is kind; you be kind.

LUKE 6:35-36 THE MESSAGE

forgive

when it comes to:

friendship

Friends love through all kinds of
weather, and families stick
together in all kinds of trouble.
PROVERBS 17:17 THE MESSAGE

Some friends may ruin you. But a real friend will be more loyal than a brother.

PROVERBS 18:24

Don't make friends with anyone who has a bad temper. You might turn out like them and get caught in a trap.

PROVERBS 22:24-25 CEV

A truly good friend will openly correct you. You can trust a friend who corrects you, but kisses from an enemy are nothing but lies.

PROVERBS 27:5-6 CEV

friendship

when I feel:

frustrated

Be brave. Be strong. Don't give up.
Expect God to get here soon.
PSALM 31:24 THE MESSAGE

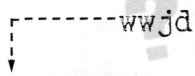

I pray that the God who gives hope will fill you with much joy and peace while you trust in him. Then your hope will overflow by the power of the Holy Spirit.

ROMANS 15:13

Wait and trust the Lord. Don't be upset when others get rich or when someone else's plans succeed.

PSALM 37:7

Weapons made to attack you won't be successful; words spoken against you won't hurt at all.

ISAIAH 54:17 CEV

frustrated

when tempted with:

gossip

I [God] put a gag on the gossip who bad-mouths his neighbor; I can't stand arrogance.

PSALM 101:5 THE MESSAGE

Lord, help me control my tongue.
Help me be careful about what I
say.

PSALM 141:3

I promise you that on the day of
judgment, everyone will have to
account for every careless word
they have spoken. On that day
they will be told that they are
either innocent or guilty because
of the things they have said.

MATTHEW 12:36-37 CEV

When you talk, do not say harmful
things. But say what people need—
words that will help others become
stronger. Then what you say will
help those who listen to you.

EPHESIANS 4:29

gossip

when I need:

guidance

If you don't know what you're doing, pray to the Father. He loves to help. You'll get his help, and won't be condescended to when you ask for it.

JAMES 1:5 THE MESSAGE

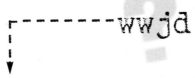

You said to me, "I will point out the road that you should follow. I will be your teacher and watch over you."

PSALM 3 2:8 CEV

Your word is like a lamp for my feet and a light for my way.

PSALM 1 1 9:105

Obey the teaching of your parents — always keep it in mind and never forget it. Their teaching will guide you when you walk, protect you when you sleep, and talk to you when you are awake.

PROVERBS 6:2 0-2 2 CEV

guidance

if I'm tempted with:

impure thoughts

We destroy every proud thing that raises itself against the knowledge of God. We capture every thought and make it give up and obey Christ.

2 CORINTHIANS 10:5

wwjd

Laura

Summing it all up, friends, I'd say
you'll do best by filling your
minds and meditating on things
true, noble, reputable, authentic,
compelling, gracious—the best,
not the worst; the beautiful, not
the ugly; things to praise, not
things to curse.

PHILIPPIANS 4:8 THE MESSAGE

Get rid of these evil thoughts and
ask God to forgive you.

ACTS 8:2 2 CEV

God, we come into your Temple.
There we think about your love.

PSALM 48:9

impure thoughts

if I'm tempted with:

jealousy

Whenever people are jealous or selfish, they cause trouble and do all sorts of cruel things.

JAMES 3:16 CEV

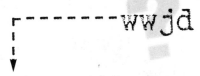

We get our new life from the
Spirit. So we should follow the
Spirit. We must not be proud. We
must not make trouble with each
other. And we must not be jealous
of each other.

GALATIANS 5:25-26

Do not want anything that
belongs to someone else.

EXODUS 20:17 CEV

Don't be jealous of men who use
violence. And don't choose to be
like them.

PROVERBS 3:31

jealousy

if I need:

joy

WWJD

So you will go out with joy. You
will be lead out in peace. The
mountains and hills will burst
into song before you. All the trees
in the fields will clap their hands.

ISAIAH 55:12

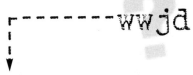

Blessed are the people who know
the passwords of praise, who
shout on parade in the bright
presence of God. Delighted, they
dance all day long; they know
who you are, what you do—they
can't keep it quiet!

PSALM 89:15-16 THE MESSAGE

Nehemiah said, "Go and enjoy
good food and sweet drinks. Send
some to people who have none.
Today is a holy day to the Lord.
Don't be sad. The joy of the Lord
will make you strong."

NEHEMIAH 8:10

You make our hearts glad because
we trust you, the only God.

PSALM 33:21 CEV

joy

if I need:

knowledge

If a person pleases God, God will give him wisdom, knowledge and joy.

ECCLESIASTES 2:26

wwjd

You will make his people know
that they will be saved by having
their sins forgiven.

LUKE 1:77

Each of you is now a new person.
You are becoming more and more
like your Creator, and you will
understand him better.

COLOSSIANS 3:10 CEV

I want you woven into a tapestry
of love, in touch with everything
there is to know of God. Then you
will have minds confident and at
rest, focused on Christ, God's great
mystery. All the richest treasures
of wisdom and knowledge are
embedded in that mystery and
nowhere else.

COLOSSIANS 2:2-3 THE MESSAGE

knowledge

when I'm tempted by:

laziness

Our first duty is to be faithful to
the one we work for.

1 CORINTHIANS 4:2 CEV

Do you see a man skilled in his work? The man will work for kings. He won't have to work for ordinary people.

PROVERBS 22:29

Sloth makes you poor; diligence brings wealth.

PROVERBS 10:4 THE MESSAGE

Lazy people sleep a lot. Idle people will go hungry.

PROVERBS 19:15

No matter how much you want, laziness won't help a bit, but hard work will reward you more than enough.

PROVERBS 13:4 CEV

laziness

if I feel:

lonely

Those who know the Lord trust him. He will not leave those who come to him.

PSALM 9:10

God assured us, "I'll never let you down, never walk off and leave you."

HEBREWS 13:5 THE MESSAGE

The eternal God is our hiding place; he carries us in his arms.

DEUTERONOMY 33:27 CEV

None of this fazes us because Jesus loves us. I'm absolutely convinced that nothing — nothing living or dead, angelic or demonic, today or tomorrow, high or low, thinkable or unthinkable — absolutely nothing can get between us and God's love because of the way that Jesus our Master has embraced us.

ROMANS 8:37-39 THE MESSAGE

lonely

if I need to walk in:

love

So these three things continue forever: faith, hope and love. And the greatest of these is love.

1 CORINTHIANS 13:13

Pursue a righteous life—a life of
wonder, faith, love, steadiness,
courtesy.

    1 TIMOTHY 6:11 THE MESSAGE

Most important of all, you must
sincerely love each other, because
love wipes away many sins.

        1 PETER 4:8 CEV

Everything we know about God's
Word is summed up in a single
sentence: Love others as you love
yourself.

    GALATIANS 5:14 THE MESSAGE

love

when it comes to:

money/materialism

You, Lord, are my shepherd. I will never be in need.

PSALM 23:1 CEV

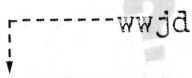

You can be sure that God will take care of everything you need, his generosity exceeding even yours in the glory that pours from Jesus.

PHILIPPIANS 4:1 9 THE MESSAGE

And God can give you more blessings than you need. Then you will always have plenty of everything. You will have enough to give to every good work.

2 CORINTHIANS 9:8

Honor the Lord! You are his special people. No one who honors the Lord will ever be in need.

PSALM 3 4:9 CEV

money/materialism

when it comes to:

music/media

Happy is the person who doesn't listen to the wicked. He doesn't go where sinners go. He doesn't do what bad people do. He loves the Lord's teachings. He thinks about those teachings day and night.

PSALM 1:1-2

wwjd

Finally, my friends, keep your minds on whatever is true, pure, right, holy, friendly, and proper. Don't ever stop thinking about what is truly worthwhile and worthy of praise.

PHILIPPIANS 4:8 CEV

Always set a good example for others.

TITUS 2:7 CEV

We use our powerful God-tools for smashing warped philosophies, tearing down barriers erected against the truth of God, fitting every loose thought and emotion and impulse into the structure of life shaped by Christ.

2 CORINTHIANS 10:5 THE MESSAGE

music/media

If I need:

patience

My brothers, you will have many kinds of troubles. But when these things happen, you should be very happy. You know that these things are testing your faith. And this will give you patience.

JAMES 1:2-3

Something completed is better than something just begun; patience is better than too much pride.

ECCLESIASTES 7:8 CEV

We do not want you to become lazy. Be like those who have faith and patience. They will receive what God has promised.

HEBREWS 6:1 2

Be patient like those farmers and don't give up. The Lord will soon be here!

JAMES 5:8 CEV

patience

if I need:

peace

We have been made right with God because of our faith. So we have peace with God through our Lord Jesus Christ.

ROMANS 5:1

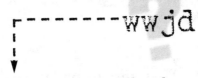

I will listen to you, Lord God,
because you promise peace to
those who are faithful and no
longer foolish.

PSALM 85:8 CEV

Those who love your teachings
will find true peace. Nothing will
defeat them.

PSALM 119:165

I give you peace, the kind of peace
that only I can give. It isn't like the
peace that this world can give. So
don't be worried or afraid.

JOHN 14:27 CEV

peace

if I'm tempted by:

peer pressure

Dear friend, if bad companions tempt you, don't go along with them.

PROVERBS 1:10 THE MESSAGE

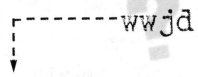
wwjd

You are not the same as those who do not believe. So do not join yourselves to them. Good and bad do not belong together. Light and darkness cannot share together.

2 CORINTHIANS 6:14

If you do the right thing, honesty will be your guide. But if you are crooked, you will be trapped by your own dishonesty.

PROVERBS 11:3 CEV

An empty-head thinks mischief is fun, but a mindful person relishes wisdom.

PROVERBS 10:23 THE MESSAGE

peer pressure

when I'm faced with:

persecution

You're blessed when your commitment to God provokes persecution. The persecution drives you even deeper into God's kingdom.

MATTHEW 5:10 THE MESSAGE

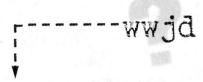

Anyone who belongs to Christ
Jesus and wants to live right will
have trouble from others.

2 TIMOTHY 3:1 2 CEV

People curse us, but we bless them.
They hurt us, and we accept it.

1 CORINTHIANS 4:1 2

We often suffer, but we are never
crushed. Even when we don't
know what to do, we never give
up. In times of trouble, God is
with us, and when we are
knocked down, we get up again.

2 CORINTHIANS 4:8-9 CEV

persecution

when it comes to:

prayer

Don't worry about anything, but pray about everything. With thankful hearts offer up your prayers and requests to God.

PHILIPPIANS 4:6 CEV

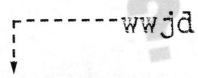

Depend on the Lord and his strength. Always go to him for help.
1 CHRONICLES 16:11

Stay alert; be in prayer so you won't wander into temptation without even knowing you're in danger.
MATTHEW 26:41 THE MESSAGE

Never give up praying. And when you pray, keep alert and be thankful.
COLOSSIANS 4:2 CEV

Pray all the time; thank God no matter what happens. This is the way God wants you who belong to Christ Jesus to live.
1 THESSALONIANS 5:17
THE MESSAGE

prayer

if I'm tempted with:

pride

The stuck-up fall flat on their faces, but down-to-earth people stand firm.

PROVERBS 11:2 THE MESSAGE

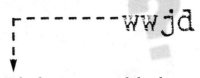

Hezekiah was so proud that he refused to thank the Lord for everything he had done for him. This made the Lord angry, and he punished Hezekiah and the people of Judah and Jerusalem. Hezekiah and the people later felt sorry and asked the Lord to forgive them. So the Lord did not punish them as long as Hezekiah was king.

2 CHRONICLES 32:25-26 CEV

If you respect the Lord, you also will hate evil. It is wise to hate pride and bragging, evil ways and lies.

PROVERBS 8:13

It is better to finish something than to start it. It is better to be patient than to be proud.

ECCLESIASTES 7:8

pride

when it comes to:

priorities

Depend on the Lord and his
strength. Always go to him for
help. Remember the wonderful
things he has done. Remember
his miracles and his decisions.

1 CHRONICLES 16:11-12

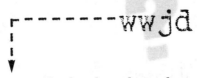

Get out of bed and get dressed!
Don't loiter and linger, waiting
until the very last minute. Dress
yourselves in Christ, and be up
and about!

ROMANS 13:14 THE MESSAGE

Whatever you say or do should be
done in the name of the Lord Jesus,
as you give thanks to God the
Father because of him.

COLOSSIANS 3:17 CEV

Self-sacrifice is the way, my way,
to finding yourself, your true self.
What kind of deal is it to get
everything you want but lose
yourself? What could you ever
trade your soul for?

MATTHEW 16:26 THE MESSAGE

priorities

if I need:

provision

This is your Father you are
dealing with, and he knows
better than you what you need.
With a God like this loving you,
you can pray very simply.

MATTHEW 6:8 THE MESSAGE

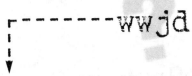

The Lord is my shepherd. I have everything I need.

PSALM 23:1

I tell you not to worry about your life. Don't worry about having something to eat, drink, or wear. Isn't life more than food or clothing? Look at the birds in the sky! They don't plant or harvest. They don't even store grain in barns. Yet your Father in heaven takes care of them. Aren't you worth more than birds?

MATTHEW 6:25-26 CEV

My God will use his wonderful riches in Christ Jesus to give you everything you need.

PHILIPPIANS 4:19

provision

if I need:

protection

Yes, because God's your refuge,
the High God your very own
home, evil can't get close to you,
harm can't get through the door.
PSALM 91:9-10 THE MESSAGE

"So no weapon that is used against you will defeat you. You will show that those who speak against you are wrong. These are the good things my servants receive. Their victory comes from me," says the Lord.

ISAIAH 54:17

In times of war and famine, God will keep you safe. You will be sheltered, without fear of hurtful words or any other weapon.

JOB 5:20-21 CEV

I can lie down and sleep soundly because you, Lord, will keep me safe.

PSALM 4:8 CEV

protection

when I'm faced with:

racism

But I am giving you a new command. You must love each other, just as I have loved you.
JOHN 13:34 CEV

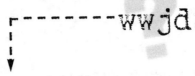

Now, in Christ, there is no
difference between Jew and
Greek. There is no difference
between slaves and free men.
There is no difference between
male and female. You are all the
same in Christ Jesus.

GALATIANS 3:28

Do as God does. After all, you are
his dear children. Let love be your
guide. Christ loved us and offered
his life as a sacrifice that pleases
God.

EPHESIANS 5:1-2 CEV

The Lord treats everyone the
same.

COLOSSIANS 3:25

racism

when it comes to:

reading the bible

By your words I can see where
I'm going; they throw a beam of
light on my dark path.

PSALM 119:105 THE MESSAGE

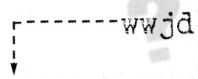

Using the Scriptures, the person who serves God will be ready and will have everything he needs to do every good work.

2 TIMOTHY 3:17

What God has said isn't only alive and active! It is sharper than any double-edged sword.

HEBREWS 4:1 2 CEV

Every word of God can be trusted. He protects those who come to him for safety.

PROVERBS 3 0:5

How can a young person live a pure life? He can do it by obeying your word.

PSALM 1 1 9:9

reading the bible

when I'm faced with:

rejection

Friends come and friends go, but a true friend sticks by you like family.

PROVERBS 18:24 THE MESSAGE

Before the world was created, God
had Christ choose us to live with
him and to be his holy and
innocent and loving people. God
was kind and decided that Christ
would choose us to be God's own
adopted children.

EPHESIANS 1:4-5 CEV

God will never walk away from
his people, never desert his
precious people.

PSALM 94:14 THE MESSAGE

I told you these things so that you
can have peace in me. In this world
you will have trouble. But be
brave! I have defeated the world!

JOHN 16:33

rejection

when it comes to:

relationships

But if we walk in the light, God
himself being the light, we also
experience a shared life with one
another, as the sacrificed blood of
Jesus, God's Son, purges all our sin.
1 JOHN 1:7 THE MESSAGE

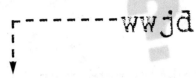

Children, obey your parents the way the Lord wants. This is the right thing to do. The command says, "Honor your father and mother." This is the first command that has a promise with it.

EPHESIANS 6:1-2

A friend is always a friend, and relatives are born to share our troubles.

PROVERBS 17:17 CEV

Don't forget your friend or your father's friend. Don't always go to your brother for help when trouble comes. A neighbor close by is better than a brother far away.

PROVERBS 27:10

relationships

when tempted with:

sarcasm

Let my words and my thoughts be pleasing to you, Lord, because you are my mighty rock and my protector.

PSALM 19:14 CEV

wwjd?

A gentle response defuses anger, but a sharp tongue kindles a temper-fire.

PROVERBS 15:1 THE MESSAGE

A wise person is known for his understanding. He wins people to his side with pleasant words.

PROVERBS 16:21

Gracious speech is like clover honey—good taste to the soul, quick energy for the body.

PROVERBS 16:24 THE MESSAGE

Rash language cuts and maims, but there is healing in the words of the wise.

PROVERBS 12:18 THE MESSAGE

sarcasm

if I need:

self-control

Do your best to improve your faith. You can do this by adding goodness, understanding, self-control, patience, devotion to God, concern to others, and love.

2 PETER 1:5-6 CEV

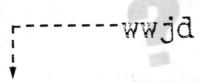

Control yourselves and be careful!
The devil is your enemy. And he
goes around like a roaring lion
looking for someone to eat.

1 PETER 5:8

But we belong to the day; so we
should control ourselves. We
should wear faith and love to
protect us. And the hope of
salvation should be our helmet.

1 THESSALONIANS 5:8

God's Spirit makes us loving,
happy, peaceful, patient, kind,
good, faithful, gentle, and self-
controlled. There is no law against
behaving in any of these ways.

GALATIANS 5:22-23 CEV

self-control

if I need:

self-discipline

Dear friends, God is good. So I beg you to offer your bodies to him as a living sacrifice, pure and pleasing. That's the most sensible way to serve God.

ROMANS 12:1 CEV

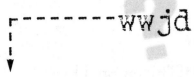

The life you see me living is not "mine," but it is lived by faith in the Son of God, who loved me and gave himself for me.

GALATIANS 2:20 THE MESSAGE

We know that our old life died with Christ on the cross. This was so that our sinful selves would have no power over us, and we would not be slaves to sin. Anyone who has died is made free from sin's control.

ROMANS 6:6

Let the Spirit change your way of thinking and make you into a new person. You were created to be like God, and so you must please him and be truly holy.

EPHESIANS 4:23-24 CEV

self-discipline

if I'm tempted by:

self-pity

Whatever I have, wherever I am, I can make it through anything in the One who makes me who I am.
PHILIPPIANS 4:1 3 THE MESSAGE

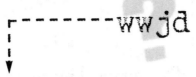

It is true that serving God makes a
person very rich, if he is satisfied
with what he has. When we came
into the world, we brought
nothing. And when we die, we
can take nothing out. So, if we
have food and clothes, we will be
satisfied with that.

1 TIMOTHY 6:6-8

Every day is hard for those who
suffer. But a happy heart makes it
like a continual feast.

PROVERBS 15:15

Trust the Lord and his mighty
power. Worship him always.
Remember his miracles and all his
wonders and his fair decisions.

1 CHRONICLES 16:11-12 CEV

self-pity

if I'm tempted by:

sexual pressure

If you hide your sins, you will not succeed. If you confess and reject them, you will receive mercy.

PROVERBS 28:13

We must not pursue the kind of sex that avoids commitment and intimacy, leaving us more lonely than ever—the kind of sex that can never "become one."

1 CORINTHIANS 6:17 THE MESSAGE

So run away from sexual sin. Every other sin that a man does is outside his body. But the one who sins sexually sins against his own body.

1 CORINTHIANS 6:18

Even if you think you can stand up to temptation, be careful not to fall.... But God can be trusted not to let you be tempted too much, and he will show you how to escape from your temptations.

1 CORINTHIANS 10:12-13 CEV

sexual pressure

when it comes to:

spiritual growth

Let the wonderful kindness and
the understanding that come from
our Lord and Savior Jesus Christ
help you to keep on growing.
2 PETER 3:18 CEV

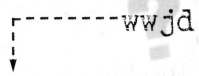

As newborn babies want milk, you should want the pure and simple teaching. By it you can grow up and be saved.

1 PETER 2:2

So come on, let's leave the preschool fingerpainting exercises on Christ and get on with the grand work of art. Grow up in Christ.

HEBREWS 6:1 THE MESSAGE

I pray that Christ will live in your hearts because of your faith. I pray that your life will be strong in love and be built on love.

EPHESIANS 3:17

if I need:

stability

Sky and earth will wear out; my
words won't wear out.

MATTHEW 24:35 THE MESSAGE

You have been born again. This new life did not come from something that dies, but from something that cannot die. You were born again through God's living message that continues forever.

1 PETER 1:23

Our Lord, you are eternal! Your word will last as long as the heavens.

PSALM 119:89 CEV

"The grass dies, and the flowers fall. But the Word of our God will live forever."

ISAIAH 40:8

stability

if I need:

strength

God makes his people strong.
God gives his people peace.
PSALM 29:11 THE MESSAGE

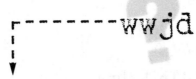

Finally, let the mighty strength of the Lord make you strong.

EPHESIANS 6:10 CEV

God's my strength, he's also my song, and now he's my salvation.

PSALM 118:14 THE MESSAGE

My body and mind may fail, but you are my strength and my choice forever.

PSALM 73:26 CEV

strength

if I'm feeling

stressed

The Lord gives perfect peace to
those whose faith is firm. So
always trust the Lord because he
is forever our mighty rock.

ISAIAH 26:3-4 CEV

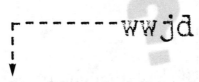

God's a safe-house for the battered,
a sanctuary during bad times. The
moment you arrive, you relax;
you're never sorry you knocked.

PSALM 9:9-10 THE MESSAGE

They will call to me, and I will
answer them. I will be with them
in trouble. I will rescue them and
honor them. I will give them a
long, full life. They will see how I
can save.

PSALM 91:15-16

It's useless to rise early and go to
bed late, and work your worried
fingers to the bone. Don't you
know he enjoys giving rest to
those he loves?

PSALM 127:2 THE MESSAGE

stressed

if I have thoughts of:

suicide

You must not murder anyone.
EXODUS 20:13

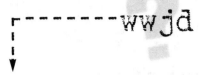

Even the hairs on your head are counted. So don't be afraid! You are worth much more than many sparrows.

MATTHEW 10:30 CEV

I praise you because of the wonderful way you created me. Everything you do is marvelous! Of this I have no doubt.

PSALM 139:14 CEV

God began doing a good work in you. And he will continue it until it is finished when Jesus Christ comes again. I am sure of that.

PHILIPPIANS 1:6

suicide

when it comes to:

swearing

Watch the way you talk. Let nothing foul or dirty come out of your mouth. Say only what helps, each word a gift.

EPHESIANS 4:2 9 THE MESSAGE

wwjd

Make your words good—you will
be glad you did. Words can bring
death or life!

PROVERBS 18:20-21 CEV

Do not misuse my name. I am the
Lord your God, and I will punish
anyone who misuses my name.

EXODUS 20:7 CEV

Fools care nothing for thoughtful
discourse; all they do is run off at
the mouth.

PROVERBS 18:2 THE MESSAGE

A person who is careful about what
he says keeps himself out of trouble.

PROVERBS 21:23

If you could find someone whose
speech was perfectly true, you'd
have a perfect person, in perfect
control of life.

JAMES 3:2 THE MESSAGE

swearing

when I'm faced with:

temptation

Stay awake and pray that you will not be tempted. Your spirit wants to do what is right, but your body is weak.

MARK 14:38

Take everything the Master has set out for you, well-made weapons of the best materials. And put them to use so you will be able to stand up to everything the Devil throws your way.

EPHESIANS 6:1 1 THE MESSAGE

Control yourselves and be careful! The devil is your enemy. And he goes around like a roaring lion looking for someone to eat. Refuse to give in to the devil. Stand strong in your faith.

1 PETER 5:8-9

Surrender to God! Resist the devil, and he will run from you.

JAMES 4:7 CEV

temptation

if I'm faced with:

tragedy

I may walk through valleys as dark as death, but I won't be afraid. You are with me, and your shepherd's rod makes me feel safe.

PSALM 23:4 CEV

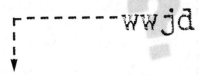

When you pass through the waters, I will be with you. When you cross rivers, you will not drown. When you walk through fire, you will not be burned. The flames will not hurt you.

ISAIAH 43:2

I will not leave you orphaned. I'm coming back.

JOHN 14:18 THE MESSAGE

You're blessed when you feel you've lost what is most dear to you. Only then can you be embraced by the One most dear to you.

MATTHEW 5:4 THE MESSAGE

tragedy

if I need:

truth

But when the Spirit of truth comes he will lead you into all truth.... He will speak only what he hears and will tell you what is to come.

JOHN 16:13

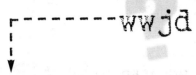

We belong to God, and everyone who knows God will listen to us. But the people who don't know God won't listen to us. That is how we can tell the Spirit that speaks the truth from the one that tells lies.

1 JOHN 4:6 CEV

The Right and Justice are the roots of your rule; Love and Truth are its fruits.

PSALM 89:14 THE MESSAGE

Plant your roots in Christ and let him be the foundation for your life. Be strong in your faith, just as you were taught. And be grateful.

COLOSSIANS 2:7 CEV

truth

when I need:

wisdom

If any of you need wisdom, you should ask God, and it will be given to you. God is generous and won't correct you for asking.

JAMES 1:5 CEV

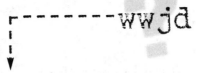

In him all the treasures of wisdom
and knowledge are safely kept.
COLOSSIANS 2:3

The wise counsel God gives
when I'm awake is confirmed by
my sleeping heart.
PSALM 16:7 THE MESSAGE

God gives out Wisdom free, is
plainspoken in Knowledge and
Understanding. He's a rich mine of
Common Sense for those who live
well, a personal bodyguard to the
candid and sincere.
PROVERBS 2:6-7 THE MESSAGE

wisdom

when I need to be a:

witness

As a tree makes fruit, a good
person gives life to others. The
wise person shows others how
to be wise.

PROVERBS 11:30

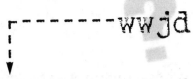

Then he told them: Go and preach
the good news to everyone in the
world. Anyone who believes me
and is baptized will be saved.

MARK 16:15-16 CEV

Everyone who has been wise will
shine as bright as the sky above,
and everyone who has led others
to please God will shine like stars.

DANIEL 12:3 CEV

But the Holy Spirit will come to
you. Then you will receive power.
You will be my witnesses—in
Jerusalem, in all of Judea, in
Samaria, and in every part of the
world.

ACTS 1:8

witness

when I'm tempted to:

worry

 Can worry make you live longer? If you don't have power over small things, why worry about everything else?

LUKE 12:25-26 CEV

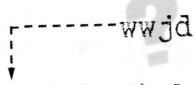

Do not worry about anything. But pray and ask God for everything you need. And when you pray, always give thanks. And God's peace will keep your hearts and minds in Christ Jesus. The peace that God gives is so great that we cannot understand it.

PHILIPPIANS 4:6-7

Pile your troubles on God's shoulders — he'll carry your load, he'll help you out. He'll never let good people topple into ruin.

PSALM 55:22 THE MESSAGE

Depend on the Lord in whatever you do. Then your plans will succeed.

PROVERBS 16:3

worry

Other items in the *WWJD* **series are**
available from your local bookstore.

WWJD portable paperback
WWJD Journal
WWJD Rocks
WWJD Keychains

Honor Books
Tulsa, Oklahoma